MW01225353

your journey through junior high life

True Reality: Your Journey Through Junior High Life
Copyright © 2004 by Antioch Media.

Requests for information should be addressed to:
Antioch Media
http://www.AntiochMedia.com/
438 E. Shaw Ave. #386
Fresno, CA 93710-7602

ISBN 0-9747772-5-0

Scripture quotations are taken from the *Holy Bible,* New Living Translation, copyright © 1996. Used by permission of Tyndale House Publishers, Inc., Wheaton, Illinois 60189. All rights reserved.

All rights reserved. No part of this publication may be reproduced, stored in a retrieval system, or transmitted in any form or by any means- electronic, mechanical, photocopy, recording, or any other- except for brief quotations in printed reviews, without the prior permission of the publisher.

Interior design by Antioch Media

Cover design by Antioch Media

Printed in the United States of America

I hope that you are ready for an adventure over the next twelve weeks. Be ready for God to move in your life like never before. This book will take you through twelve character traits, and how they can apply to your life as a junior high student.

Because everyone loves movies, we decided there would be no better way to discover the truths of the Bible than through a movie format. This book uses a simple, yet effective layout. Each chapter is broken up into seven, one-day increments. Each day is designed to give you depth without requiring much time. Let's get you familiar with the book's layout.

trailer
The trailer is designed to setup an interest in the chapter while acting as an introduction.

preview
This section is designed to help you think through the purpose of what you want to learn before you actually learn it.

feature presentation
Each day features a scripture passage on the left that corresponds with the questions on the right. Each question is designed to get you to process God's Word in order to apply it to your life. In the same way, each day's questions are designed to be completed in as little as five minutes. I believe that you need to feel successful in your daily devotions, and by minimizing the time required, you will build a foundation for deeper Spiritual growth.

credits
This section is designed to be used as the application to the study you will have done over the course of the week.

recap your thoughts
These journals are designed for you to begin to practice the discipline of recording what God is teaching you in your personal walk with Christ.

talk to God
This part of the book is designed for you to write out your prayer requests.

memory verse

By focusing on one verse weekly, you will begin putting into practice what you are studying and memorizing. I feel it is extremely important for you to begin to live your faith out rather than strictly filling yourself with knowledge.

My prayer is that God will totally rock your life in a way that causes you to step up and step out for Jesus on your campus. I believe that Junior High students, like yourself, can make a difference in this world. However, you must be willing for God to use you. Don't be afraid to grow in your walk with Christ, because it is the number one coolest thing you can ever do in life. God wants to use you. Let Him.

Jeremy Tullis
JuniorHigh4u Ministry Resources

reputation

Malachi 1:11

But my name is honored by people of other nations from morning till night. All around the world they offer sweet incense and pure offerings in honor of my name. For my name is great among the nations," says the LORD Almighty.

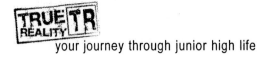
trailer

If you're like me, you care about your reputation. I mean, it matters what people think about you, how cool you look, dress, and act. Our reputation often forms our self-worth. I remember my 8th grade year. I cared so much about maintaining a cool reputation, that in order to fit in and "be cool," I went to the store and bought some extremely expensive pants. They were $70.00 to be exact! That might not sound like a lot now, but back in 1989 it was a fortune. I was so desperate to look cool, price was not an issue. In fact, color wasn't an issue either. You'd think that if I was going to spend that much money on a single pair of pants I would care about the color. Well, I didn't! The only thing I cared about was looking cool and maintaining a cool reputation at school by having the right brand on my clothing. When I arrived at school the next day after purchasing my radical pair of pants, I noticed that the opposite of what I thought was going to happen was happening—I was being made fun of. The pants that I swore would make me cool turned me into a total geek! Why did this happen? I guess I should have cared about the color. Purple pants were not in with the cool crowd. I cared more about my reputation of being cool than anything else. I didn't care about having the reputation of being a Christ follower, a truthful person, or a fair person. All I cared about was being accepted! God wants us to care about our reputation. In fact, He wants us to have a true reputation for Him! He doesn't care about how cool we are; God just wants our hearts and lives!

preview

- How would you define true reputation?

first things first

Beginning with the end in mind helps you think through the purpose of what you want to learn before you actually learn it.

- What concerns you most, having a cool reputation with the "in" crowd, or a good reputation uplifting Christ? Why?

feature presentation

This week we are discussing what a true reputation for Christ looks likes. We want to ask ourselves this question, "How is a good reputation built?" To answer this question, we will dive into the word of God and check out how God wants our reputations built. Before moving forward, though, stop and ask God to break your heart. Ask Him to invade your reality right now and show you what your reputation is built upon. Then ask for His strength to mold and shape your life over this week as you focus on developing a true reputation for Christ.

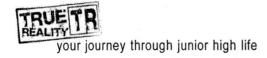
day one

Read **Deuteronomy 4:1-2**.

- What does Moses say God requires all of us to do in these verses?

> "And now, Israel, listen carefully to these laws and regulations that I am about to teach you. Obey them so that you may live, so you may enter and occupy the land the LORD, the God of your ancestors, is giving you. Do not add to or subtract from these commands I am giving you from the LORD your God. Just obey them.
>
> -Deuteronomy 4:1-2

- What are some ways we break God's commands?

- How does developing a true reputation for Christ have anything to do with keeping God's commands?

- What does the beginning of the passage say will happen if we follow God's laws and teachings?

your thoughts

_____
_____
_____
_____
_____
_____
_____
_____
_____
_____
_____
_____
_____

If you are true in character, you are able to combat any attack the Devil sends your way.

talk to God

_____
_____
_____
_____
_____
_____
_____
_____
_____
_____
_____
_____

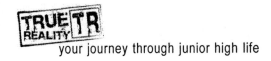
day two

Check out **Deuteronomy 4:3-5**.

- In verse 3, why does Moses bring up the incident with Baal (Baal was an idol people worshiped)?

You saw what the LORD did to you at Baal-peor, where the LORD your God destroyed everyone who had worshiped the god Baal of Peor. But all of you who were faithful to the LORD your God are still alive today. "You must obey these laws and regulations when you arrive in the land you are about to enter and occupy. The LORD my God gave them to me and commanded me to pass them on to you.

-Deuteronomy 4:3-5

- If we cling to God as the one we find our identity in, how does that help us build an true reputation?

- God doesn't just call each of us to know His commands and teachings. What else does he want His children to do?

- Do you find it hard to live for God at school? Why/why not? Would your friends say that you have a true reputation?

your thoughts

_____

_____

_____

_____

_____

_____

_____

_____

_____

_____

_____

The enemy desires that you think the task of sharing the Good News with others is a worthless and hopeless task.

talk to God

_____

_____

_____

_____

_____

_____

_____

_____

_____

_____

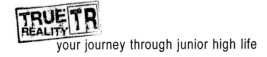
day three

Read **Deuteronomy 4:6-9**.

- What happens in this passage?

> If you obey them carefully, you will display your wisdom and intelligence to the surrounding nations. When they hear about these laws, they will exclaim, 'What other nation is as wise and prudent as this!' For what great nation has a god as near to them as the LORD our God is near to us whenever we call on him? And what great nation has laws and regulations as fair as this body of laws that I am giving you today? "But watch out! Be very careful never to forget what you have seen the LORD do for you. Do not let these things escape from your mind as long as you live! And be sure to pass them on to your children and grandchildren.
>
> -Deuteronomy 4:6-9

- What radical things has God done in your life over the 11-14 years you've been alive?

- How does never forgetting the awesomeness of God in our lives help us to build a true reputation?

your thoughts

_____
_____
_____
_____
_____
_____
_____
_____
_____
_____
_____
_____
_____

Only by memorizing God's Word are you able to use it as a sword in battle.

talk to God

_____
_____
_____
_____
_____
_____
_____
_____
_____
_____
_____

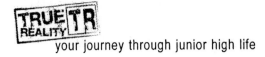
day four

Read **Deuteronomy 4:10-14**.

- According to this passage, how is a true reputation built?

  HINT: The answer won't jump out and bite you, you must look into the verses meaning to fully understand.

Tell them especially about the day when you stood before the LORD your God at Mount Sinai, where he told me, 'Summon the people before me, and I will instruct them. That way, they will learn to fear me as long as they live, and they will be able to teach my laws to their children.' You came near and stood at the foot of the mountain, while the mountain was burning with fire. Flames shot into the sky, shrouded in black clouds and deep darkness. And the LORD spoke to you from the fire. You heard his words but didn't see his form; there was only a voice. He proclaimed his covenant, which he commanded you to keep – the Ten Commandments – and wrote them on two stone tablets. It was at that time that the LORD commanded me to issue the laws and regulations you must obey in the land you are about to enter and occupy.

-Deuteronomy 4:10-14

- How does following God's rules for our lives build a true reputation?

- What kind of reputation does God want each of His children to possess?

- Is God only concerned that we follow the Ten Commandments or are there other commands in the Bible we must also obey? If so, what are they?

your thoughts

_____

_____

_____

_____

_____

_____

_____

_____

_____

_____

_____

_____

_____

_____

_____

If the devil can cause you to focus on your own selfish desires, he has won the battle.

talk to God

_____

_____

_____

_____

_____

_____

_____

_____

_____

_____

_____

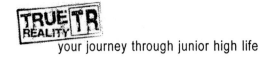
credits

- After completing this lesson, what does a true reputation look like to you now?

The credits section is designed to help you apply this week's chapter to your life. It can also be used for further discussion in a small group setting.

- What must you focus on in order to begin developing a true reputation for God?

- Do you think people at your school will make fun of you for following Christ? Why/why not?

- Are you willing to accept the challenge of turning other's eyes toward God rather than turning people's eyes at your school on yourself? If so, list the ways you will begin to do this.

your thoughts

_____
_____
_____
_____
_____
_____
_____
_____
_____
_____
_____
_____
_____
_____

talk to God

As a Christian, you are called by God to stand out and be different from the rest of the world.

_____
_____
_____
_____
_____
_____
_____
_____
_____
_____
_____
_____
_____

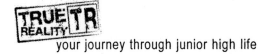
day six

memory verse

- What are some key things to remember about having a true reputation?

But my name is honored by people of other nations from morning till night. All around the world they offer sweet incense and pure offerings in honor of my name. For my name is great among the nations," says the LORD Almighty.

-Malachi 1:11

- What is one thing I will commit to the Lord this week?

your thoughts

_____
_____
_____
_____
_____
_____
_____
_____
_____
_____
_____
_____

If you are truly serious about making a difference in your world for Christ, you must first understand and practice true character.

talk to God

_____
_____
_____
_____
_____
_____
_____
_____
_____
_____

day seven

review

- What has God promised me this week?

keeping it real

Having a true reputation allows us to experience the fulness of what God desires for us.

Take some time to answer these questions. It may not seem important now, but it will be awesome to look back and see how God has shaped your life.

- Does God have a command for me to obey?

- Have I done anything that I need forgiveness from God for?

- What lesson does God want me to remember this week?

- Questions about this study I need answered:

your thoughts

_____
_____
_____
_____
_____
_____
_____
_____
_____
_____
_____
_____

talk to God

God desires each Christian to know His Word and memorize it.

_____
_____
_____
_____
_____
_____
_____
_____
_____
_____
_____

integrity

weekly verse

1 Samuel 16:7

But the LORD said to Samuel, "Don't judge by his appearance or height, for I have rejected him. The LORD doesn't make decisions the way you do! People judge by outward appearance, but the LORD looks at a person's thoughts and intentions."

trailer

During my college years I worked as an "environmental engineer." For those of you who do not know what that is, I'll simplify for you. It's a janitor! That's right; you're not seeing things, a janitor. I cleaned dirty toilets and people's vomit. I mopped floors, vacuumed carpets, picked up office spaces, windexed windows, and painted walls. I was put into many situations that were uncomfortable and down right gross! However, the thing I remember most about my job was the trust factor. My boss had tons of trust in me and my ability to get the job done right the first time. I cleaned a large church and my shift went late into the night long after meetings let out. I would often be there alone without any supervision. I know this sounds like a dream job for many of you reading, and in many ways it was. I did, however, take my job seriously. I knew that my boss, the church staff, the congregation, and God put loads of trust me. I was not about to let everyone down. I did my job, whatever the task, with competence and integrity. In fact, I had many people compliment me for doing my job with true integrity. I knew that in everything I did I represented God. Therefore I wanted to do my absolute best whether someone was watching me or not! I am so glad that I decided to represent God by maintaining true integrity through all the difficulties that the job entailed. And, although I no longer clean toilets for a living, that job allowed me to develop an understanding that regardless of one's job, God requires His children to model their life after His. God wants each of us to do the right thing, even when there is no one watching. This is called true integrity.

preview

- What does true integrity mean to you?

first things first

Beginning with the end
in mind helps you think
through the purpose of
what you want to
learn before you
actually learn it.

- Define integrity in your own words.

- Why is maintaining a high level of true integrity so important?

- Would your friends, parents, and teachers say that you are a person of true integrity? Why/why not?

feature presentation

This week we are discussing what it takes to maintain true integrity for Christ in all we do. God has called each of us as His children to a higher standard of living. Although the world tells us that it is okay to cheat, lie, and steal to get what we "deserve," God's word says otherwise! We are called to live a life that is above reproach, a life full of true integrity! Before you go any further, and ask God to show you where you need to step up your level of integrity. Ask God to give you the desire and willingness to become a person known for true integrity.

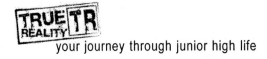

day one

Read **1 Samuel 16:7.**

- What does God tell Samuel not to judge?

> But the LORD said to Samuel, "Don't judge by his appearance or height, for I have rejected him. The LORD doesn't make decisions the way you do! People judge by outward appearance, but the LORD looks at a person's thoughts and intentions."
>
> -1 Samuel 16:7

- Why is it so important for us as Christians not to judge an outward appearance?

- Does integrity have anything to do with our heart? If so, what?

your thoughts

_____
_____
_____
_____
_____
_____
_____
_____
_____
_____
_____
_____
_____
_____

The most difficult part of sharing your faith with your friends is asking them the first question about Jesus.

talk to God

_____
_____
_____
_____
_____
_____
_____
_____
_____
_____
_____

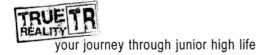

day two

Check out **2 Chronicles 26:3-4**.

- How old was Uzziah when he became king?

Uzziah was sixteen when he became king, and he reigned in Jerusalem fifty-two years. His mother was Jecoliah, from Jerusalem. He did what was pleasing in the LORD's sight, just as his father, Amaziah, had done.

-2 Chronicles 26:3-4

- Does age have anything to do with our level of integrity?

- God built up Uzziah's kingdom and gave him many successes in war because of one character trait. What is it?

- Are you a person who does what is right even when no one is watching? Be honest.

your thoughts

_____
_____
_____
_____
_____
_____
_____
_____
_____
_____
_____
_____

Christianity is the only religion that claims you can have a relationship with the One True God.

talk to God

_____
_____
_____
_____
_____
_____
_____
_____
_____
_____
_____
_____

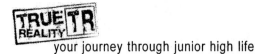
day three

Read **Psalm 101:3-5**.

- What happens in this passage?

> I will refuse to look at anything vile and vulgar. I hate all crooked dealings; I will have nothing to do with them. I will reject perverse ideas and stay away from every evil. I will not tolerate people who slander their neighbors. I will not endure conceit and pride.
>
> -Psalm 101:3-5

- What do the terms vile, vulgar, perverse, and slander mean?

- What kind of effort does it take for us to be people of true integrity?

your thoughts

talk to God

In order to know what is false, you must know and believe the truth about Jesus Christ and what He did for you on the cross.

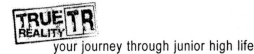
day four

Read **Psalm 101:6-8**.

• What does David the psalmist promise to do?

I will keep a protective eye on the godly, so they may dwell with me in safety. Only those who are above reproach will be allowed to serve me. I will not allow deceivers to serve me, and liars will not be allowed to enter my presence. My daily task will be to ferret out criminals and free the city of the LORD from their grip.

-Psalm 101:6-8

• How does the first part apply to our efforts of becoming people with true integrity?

• Who should we associate with and who should we not?

• According to this passage, what kind of effort does it take for us to be people of true integrity?

your thoughts

_____

_____

_____

_____

_____

_____

_____

_____

_____

_____

_____

_____

God's desire is to see each Christian live a true life for Him.

talk to God

_____

_____

_____

_____

_____

_____

_____

_____

_____

_____

_____

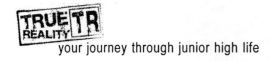
day five

credits

- After completing this lesson, what does true integrity look like to you now?

The credits section is designed to help you apply this week's chapter to your life. It can also be used for further discussion in a small group setting.

- What must you focus on in order to begin developing true integrity for God?

- How do you think people at school will respond if you become a person with true integrity?

- Are you willing to put in the effort it takes to become a person of true integrity? List the action steps you are willing to take to begin your journey.

your thoughts

_____
_____
_____
_____
_____
_____
_____
_____
_____
_____
_____
_____
_____

The enemy desires that you think the task of sharing the Good News with others is a worthless and hopeless task.

talk to God

_____
_____
_____
_____
_____
_____
_____
_____
_____
_____
_____

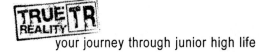
day six

memory verse

- What are some key things to remember about having a true reputation?

But the LORD said to Samuel, "Don't judge by his appearance or height, for I have rejected him. The LORD doesn't make decisions the way you do! People judge by outward appearance, but the LORD looks at a person's thoughts and intentions."

- 1 Samuel 16:7

- What is one thing I will commit to the Lord this week?

_____
_____
_____
_____
_____
_____
_____
_____
_____
_____
_____
_____
_____

If you are true in character, you are able to combat any attack the Devil sends your way.

talk to God

_____
_____
_____
_____
_____
_____
_____
_____
_____
_____
_____

day seven

review

- What has God promised me this week?

keeping it real

Having true integrity gives honor to God and allows the Holy Spirit to show through in your life!

Take some time to answer these questions. It may not seem important now, but it will be awesome to look back and see how God has shaped your life.

- Does God have a command for me to obey?

- Have I done anything that I need forgiveness from God for?

- What lesson does God want me to remember this week?

- Questions about this study I need answered:

your thoughts

_____

_____

_____

_____

_____

_____

_____

_____

_____

_____

_____

_____

_____

talk to God

Only by memorizing God's Word are you able to use it as a sword in battle.

_____

_____

_____

_____

_____

_____

_____

_____

_____

_____

_____

_____

attitude

weekly verse

Matthew 15:8-9

"...'These people honor me with their lips, but their hearts are far away. Their worship is a farce, for they replace God's commands with their own man-made teachings.'"

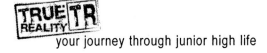

trailer

Growing up my father would say, "You need an attitude adjustment." The reason I hated hearing that so much was because I knew he was right, but I enjoyed acting like a jerk every once in a while. My attitude affected my family and friends in many ways. I remember one morning my brother and I woke up around 5:00 am to do our paper route. I was so tired and fed up with early mornings that I was a total jerk to him. I was bossy, uptight, and mean. My brother, however, just kept his mouth shut. After we were finished folding the papers, we strapped on our rollerblades and loaded each other down with the papers. During the entire time I continued to yell at my brother. My attitude stunk. As we both rolled down the driveway, my brother's patience grew thin with me and he went ballistic. He grabbed my paper bag that was around my neck and began choking me uncontrollably telling me to shut up and stop complaining. If ever there had been a time I needed an attitude adjustment, it was then. Once he shook some sense into my brain, I apologized and realized that my attitude was not Christ like. I didn't just need an attitude adjustment; I needed an attitude overhaul! I wanted everyone around to notice that there was a difference in the way I was acting and be blown away at my new true attitude for Christ. I began working on my attitude and slowly it changed. Soon people really began to notice a difference. How has your attitude been lately? Do you need an attitude adjustment or overhaul?

preview

- What does having a true attitude mean to you?

first things first

Beginning with the end in mind helps you think through the purpose of what you want to learn before you actually learn it.

- What kind of attitude would your friends say you have?

- Why should we as Christians be concerned with our attitudes?

feature presentation

This week we are discussing what it takes to maintain a true attitude for Christ. God wants each of us to do everything joyfully without complaining as if we were doing it for Him directly. Can you say that you do your schoolwork joyfully? How about your chores? Many times our attitudes are challenged by circumstances beyond our control. It is during these times especially, though, that we must choose to maintain a true attitude for Christ. Ask God to reveal to you one area in your attitude that needs to change.

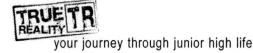

day one

Read **Matthew 15:8-9.**

- What does the first part of this passage mean?

"...'These people honor me with their lips, but their hearts are far away. Their worship is a farce, for they replace God's commands with their own man-made teachings.'"

-Matthew 15:8-9

- Define the word farce.

- What does the second part of this passage mean?

- Where does our attitude stem from?

- As Christians, do we worship God with our attitudes? How? When?

- Is our attitude a direct reflection of what's inside our heart? Explain.

your thoughts

_____
_____
_____
_____
_____
_____
_____
_____
_____
_____
_____
_____
_____

talk to God

If the devil can cause you to focus on your own selfish desires, he has won the battle.

_____
_____
_____
_____
_____
_____
_____
_____
_____
_____

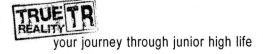

day two

Check out **Matthew 5:3-5**.

- Why does God tell us that we are blessed if we mourn?

"God blesses those who realize their need for him, for the Kingdom of Heaven is given to them. God blesses those who mourn, for they will be comforted. God blesses those who are gentle and lowly, for the whole earth will belong to them."

-Matthew 5:3-5

- What kind of attitudes are we capturing if we realize our need for God, mourn, and are gentle and lowly?

- How can we show that attitude?

your thoughts

_____
_____
_____
_____
_____
_____
_____
_____
_____
_____
_____

As a Christian, you are called by God to stand out and be different from the rest of the world.

talk to God

_____
_____
_____
_____
_____
_____
_____
_____
_____
_____

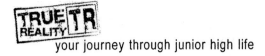

day three

Read **Matthew 5:6-8**.

- Define Righteousness in your own words.

God blesses those who are hungry and thirsty for justice, for they will receive it in full. God blesses those who are merciful, for they will be shown mercy. God blesses those whose hearts are pure, for they will see God.

-Matthew 5:6-8

- List a few ways we can show mercy to others.

- How does the end of this passage affect our attitudes?

- Are we able to develop a true attitude for Christ without first developing a pure heart? Why/why not?

_____

_____

_____

_____

_____

_____

_____

_____

_____

_____

_____

_____

_____

_____

_____

If you are truly serious about making a difference in your world for Christ, you must first understand and practice true character.

talk to God

_____

_____

_____

_____

_____

_____

_____

_____

_____

_____

_____

_____

_____

_____

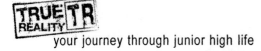

day four

Read **Matthew 5:11-12**.

- Why is it so hard to maintain a positive attitude when people at school insult us, make fun of us, and lie about us? Why do we feel we need to defend ourselves?

"God blesses you when you are mocked and persecuted and lied about because you are my followers. Be happy about it! Be very glad! For a great reward awaits you in heaven. And remember, the ancient prophets were persecuted, too."

-Matthew 5:11-12

- What does God's word say to do when this happens?

- List some honest ways we are able to rejoice when people slam us.

- Where does our true attitude come from?

your thoughts

_____
_____
_____
_____
_____
_____
_____
_____
_____
_____
_____
_____

God desires each Christian to know His Word and memorize it.

talk to God

_____
_____
_____
_____
_____
_____
_____
_____
_____
_____
_____
_____

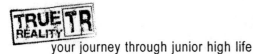
credits

- After completing this lesson, what does a true attitude look like to you now?

The credits section is designed to help you apply this week's chapter to your life. It can also be used for further discussion in a small group setting.

- What must you focus on in order to begin developing your true attitude for God?

- How do you think people at your school will respond when your attitude turns true for Christ?

- List some steps to help you begin the process of developing your positive true attitude.

your thoughts

_____

_____

_____

_____

_____

_____

_____

_____

_____

_____

_____

_____

talk to God

The most difficult part of sharing your faith with your friends is asking them the first question about Jesus.

_____

_____

_____

_____

_____

_____

_____

_____

_____

_____

_____

_____

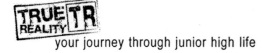
day six

memory verse

- What are some key things to remember about having a true attitude?

"...'These people honor me with their lips, but their hearts are far away. Their worship is a farce, for they replace God's commands with their own man-made teachings.'"

- Matthew 15:8 - 9

- What is one thing I will commit to the Lord this week?

your thoughts

_____

_____

_____

_____

_____

_____

_____

_____

_____

_____

_____

_____

talk to God

Christianity is the
only religion that
claims you can have
a relationship with
the One True God.

_____

_____

_____

_____

_____

_____

_____

_____

_____

_____

_____

keeping it real

Having a true attitude gives honor to God and allows the Holy Spirit to show through in your life!

Take some time to answer these questions. It may not seem important now, but it will be awesome to look back and see how God has shaped your life.

day seven

review

- What has God promised me this week?

- Does God have a command for me to obey?

- Have I done anything that I need forgiveness from God for?

- What lesson does God want me to remember this week?

- Questions about this study I need answered:

your thoughts

_____

_____

_____

_____

_____

_____

_____

_____

_____

_____

_____

talk to God

If you are true in character, you are able to combat any attack the Devil sends your way.

_____

_____

_____

_____

_____

_____

_____

_____

_____

_____

_____

honesty

weekly verse

Matthew 15:18-20

"But evil words come from an evil heart and defile the person who says them. For from the heart come evil thoughts, murder, adultery, all other sexual immorality, theft, lying, and slander. These are what defile you. . ."

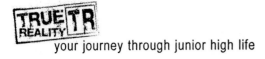

trailer

Have you ever been caught in a lie? How did it make you feel? Did you feel like you had let someone down? I remember back to when I was in 5th grade. Class had just let out and it was time for lunch. I was so excited because I loved to eat. This was the one subject I really looked forward to. Now this particular day started off normally. My friends and I walked into the cafeteria, sat down, and opened our lunch pails (They were in back then. You guys totally miss out now). No sooner had I opened my lunch pail, when I got this strong urge to throw something. Since the only thing around me was food, I hurled half my peanut butter and jelly sandwich across the cafeteria nailing this chick in the back of the head. My friends caught on and began tossing their food too. It only took a few minutes and the entire cafeteria was out of control. Food, drinks, lunch pails, shoes, anything that could be thrown was and all because of my urge. Well you guessed it, I was taken into the principal's office and asked a very straight forward question, "Did you start or have anything to do with the food fight in the cafeteria today"? Being the extremely honest person I was, I replied, "No, I have no idea what you're talking about." Finally, I broke down and admitted my guilt. I received detention for a week and had to clean up the school grounds. The food fight was totally worth my punishment, but looking back I regret having lied to my principal. See, I was a Christian and I knew what I was doing was wrong, but I chose to do it anyway. God didn't like that! As Christians, if we are going to maintain a high character, with a strong reputation as a person of integrity, we must first begin with being honest. We cannot have any of the other true Godly character traits without first maintaining a high level of true honesty.

preview

- What is true honesty to you?

first things first

Beginning with the end in mind helps you think through the purpose of what you want to learn before you actually learn it.

- Are you an honest person? Why/why not?

- Why is maintaining a high level of true honesty so important?

- Would your friends, parents, and teachers say that you are a person of true honesty? Why/why not?

feature presentation

This week we are discussing what it takes to maintain true honesty for Christ in all we do. God wants each of us to make our yes be yes and our no be no. All this means is that God does not want us to lie. He wants what comes out of our mouths to be the truth. This is what true honesty means. Ask God to help you access how honest you really are. Then, ask for God's help to make you into a person who builds their life on this principle of true honesty.

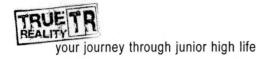

day one

Read **Exodus 20:16.**

- Write the verse below.

Do not testify falsely against your neighbor.

-Exodus 20:16

- In your own words, what is this verse talking about?

- Why is lying such a big deal to God?

- Do you believe all lies are equal in God's eyes? Why/why not?

your thoughts

_____

_____

_____

_____

_____

_____

_____

_____

_____

_____

_____

God's desire is to
see each Christian
live a true life for Him.

talk to God

_____

_____

_____

_____

_____

_____

_____

_____

_____

_____

_____

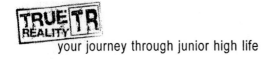
day two

Check out **Ezekiel 45:9-10**.

- What happens in this passage?

For this is what the Sovereign LORD says: Enough, you princes of Israel! Stop all your violence and oppression and do what is just and right. Quit robbing and cheating my people out of their land! Stop expelling them from their homes! You must use only honest weights and scales, honest dry volume measures, and honest liquid volume measures.

-Ezekiel 45:9-10

- What are these people doing wrong?

- Would you consider this a dishonest act? Why/why not?

your thoughts

_____

_____

_____

_____

_____

_____

_____

_____

_____

_____

_____

The enemy desires that you think the task of sharing the Good News with others is a worthless and hopeless task.

talk to God

_____

_____

_____

_____

_____

_____

_____

_____

_____

_____

_____

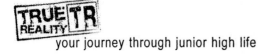

day three

Try to understand **Ezekiel 45:11-12**.

- Why is this so important?

The homer will be your standard unit for measuring volume. The ephah and the bath will each measure one-tenth of a homer. The standard unit for weight will be the silver shekel. One shekel consists of twenty gerahs, and sixty shekels are equal to one mina.

-Ezekiel 45:11-12

- What dishonesty was happening in the passage yesterday that caused this standard to be set?

Did you know? Greed and obtaining possessions with force were the two major social sins of the nation during this time. God needed to command the princes and the people to be just and right in all of their business dealings. God did not like to see people take advantage of others. God wants us to be honest. That means if our teacher says we can have free time once we have worked on our homework for thirty minutes, follow through on your end of the bargain. Give your best and just be honest!

- Is it hard for us to be honest when dealing with money? Why/why not?

your thoughts

_____

_____

_____

_____

_____

_____

_____

_____

_____

_____

_____

_____

_____

If the devil can cause you to focus on your own selfish desires, he has won the battle.

talk to God

_____

_____

_____

_____

_____

_____

_____

_____

_____

_____

_____

_____

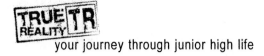
day four

Read **Matthew 15:18-20**.

- What are these verses saying?

But evil words come from an evil heart and defile the person who says them. For from the heart come evil thoughts, murder, adultery, all other sexual immorality, theft, lying, and slander. These are what defile you. Eating with unwashed hands could never defile you and make you unacceptable to God!"

-Matthew 15:18-20

- Where do evil thoughts, murder, adultery, sexual immorality, theft, and slander come from?

- What does this passage mean when it says 'defile'?

- Where does true honesty come from?

your thoughts

_____
_____
_____
_____
_____
_____
_____
_____
_____
_____
_____

talk to God

As a Christian, you are called by God to stand out and be different from the rest of the world.

_____
_____
_____
_____
_____
_____
_____
_____
_____
_____

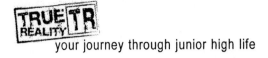
credits

- After completing this lesson, what does true honesty look like to you now?

The credits section is designed to help you apply this week's chapter to your life. It can also be used for further discussion in a small group setting.

- What must you focus on in order to begin developing true honesty for God?

- How do you think people at your school will respond when you become a person of true honesty?

- Write out a prayer asking God for Him to help you become a person of true honesty.

your thoughts

_____

_____

_____

_____

_____

_____

_____

_____

_____

_____

_____

_____

talk to God

God desires each Christian to know His Word and memorize it.

_____

_____

_____

_____

_____

_____

_____

_____

_____

_____

_____

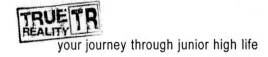
day six

memory verse

- What are some key things to remember about being truly honest?

"But evil words come from an evil heart and defile the person who says them. For from the heart come evil thoughts, murder, adultery, all other sexual immorality, theft, lying, and slander. These are what defile you. . ."

- Matthew 15:18-20

- What is one thing I will commit to the Lord this week?

your thoughts

_____
_____
_____
_____
_____
_____
_____
_____
_____
_____
_____
_____
_____
_____

talk to God

Only by memorizing God's Word are you able to use it as a sword in battle.

_____
_____
_____
_____
_____
_____
_____
_____
_____
_____
_____
_____

day seven

review

- What has God promised me this week?

keeping it real

Having true honesty can be far more rewarding than giving in to the pressures of lying, cheating, and stealing.

Take some time to answer these questions. It may not seem important now, but it will be awesome to look back and see how God has shaped your life.

- Does God have a command for me to obey?

- Have I done anything that I need forgiveness from God for?

- What lesson does God want me to remember this week?

- Questions about this study I need answered:

your thoughts

_____

_____

_____

_____

_____

_____

_____

_____

_____

_____

_____

_____

talk to God

The most difficult part of sharing your faith with your friends is asking them the first question about Jesus.

_____

_____

_____

_____

_____

_____

_____

_____

_____

_____

anger

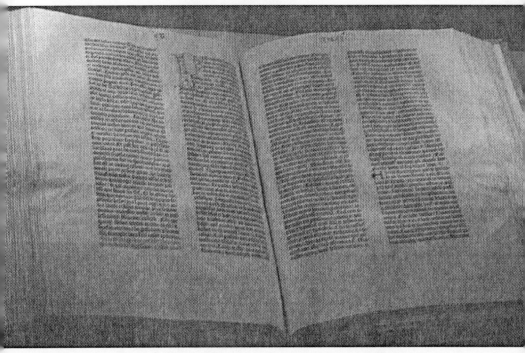

weekly verse

Ephesians 4:26-27

And "don't sin by letting anger gain control over you." Don't let the sun go down while you are still angry, for anger gives a mighty foothold to the Devil.

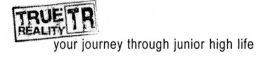
trailer

When I was a sophomore (10th grade) in high school, there was this girl who was totally obsessed with me. She was a freshman who demanded my attention 24/7. Have you ever known someone like that? During the middle of the school year she wrote me this note. I read it and told her I did not want any more notes from her; in fact, I did not want her hanging around talking to me either. I was totally fed up with this girl. She was a leech. Every time I turned my head, there she was. I felt like in many ways this "chick" was stalking me. One day, I couldn't take it any more. She wrote me this extremely sappy love note. Since she had not listened to my previous request to stop writing me notes, I decided to take matters into my own hands and ensure this would never happen again. I took her love note to the library and began to make copies. I made hundreds of copies; however I did not stop there, but proceeded to post the note all around school where every single person could read it. I was so upset that she hadn't listened to me that I didn't care how badly I hurt her. To make a long story short, I was called into my learning director's office, where this girl and I battled out our differences. In the end, I forgave her and she forgave me, but I cannot stop thinking about how my anger got the best of me. My actions not only embarrassed this girl, but totally devalued her as a person. Because of my anger, I sinned against God and against this girl. One thing I learned through this entire experience was that no matter how mad a person makes us, we are never given the right to slam or devalue another human-being. It is okay to get angry, but in our anger we must be careful not to sin.

preview

- When have you been most upset? What happened?

first things first

Beginning with the end in mind helps you think through the purpose of what you want to learn before you actually learn it.

- Do you think that it is ever okay to get angry? If so, when?

feature presentation

This week we are discussing how Christians should behave when they are filled with anger. God does not tell us that it is wrong to get angry. In fact, it is a normal human emotion. However, the actions and words that follow our anger is what we have to guard most. Ask God to reveal to you any situations this past month when your anger got the best of you. Ask God for forgiveness. Pray that He will show you the proper actions to take next time you become filled with anger.

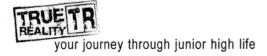
day one

Read **Ephesians 4:26-27.**

- What are some ways we can sin when we get angry?

> **And "don't sin by letting anger gain control over you." Don't let the sun go down while you are still angry, for anger gives a mighty foothold to the Devil.**
>
> -Ephesians 4:26-27

- What are some steps we can take to guard ourselves from sinning when we become angry?

- What does it mean: "Do not let the sun go down while you are still angry"? Explain.

- What is a foothold?

your thoughts

_____

_____

_____

_____

_____

_____

_____

_____

_____

_____

_____

_____

Christianity is the only religion that claims you can have a relationship with the One True God.

talk to God

_____

_____

_____

_____

_____

_____

_____

_____

_____

_____

_____

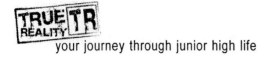
day two

Check out **John 2:13-14**.

- What does this verse say?

And the Jews' Passover was at hand, and Jesus went up to Jerusalem and found in the temple those who sold oxen and sheep and doves, and also the changers of money, sitting there.

-John 2:13-14

- What did Jesus find in the temple?

Did you know? The temple was in Jerusalem and was always crowded during Passover. The religious leaders thought it would be a good idea to let merchants set up booths to sell goods. They rationalized their actions by saying it was a convenience to the worshippers and helped raise money for the upkeep of the temple. However, there's one minor problem! The fact that it was difficult for the people to worship God due to the "flee market" didn't seem to bother the religious leaders—I mean, hey, they were making bank!

- How did this make Him feel?

- Why would Jesus be mad about people selling things and exchanging money?

your thoughts

_____

_____

_____

_____

_____

_____

_____

_____

_____

_____

_____

_____

talk to God

In order to know what is false, you must know and believe the truth about Jesus Christ and what He did for you on the cross.

_____

_____

_____

_____

_____

_____

_____

_____

_____

_____

_____

_____

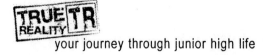
day three

Read **John 2:15-16**.

- Why does Jesus become angry?

> Jesus made a whip from some ropes and chased them all out of the Temple. He drove out the sheep and oxen, scattered the money changers' coins over the floor, and turned over their tables. Then, going over to the people who sold doves, he told them, "Get these things out of here. Don't turn my Father's house into a marketplace!"
>
> -John 2:15-16

- What does Jesus do in His anger? Does He sin? Explain.

- How can our anger give the devil a foothold?

- What is one way you will apply this passage today at school?

your thoughts

_____

_____

_____

_____

_____

_____

_____

_____

_____

_____

_____

_____

_____

God's desire is to see each Christian live a true life for Him.

talk to God

_____

_____

_____

_____

_____

_____

_____

_____

_____

_____

_____

_____

_____

_____

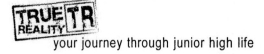
day four

Read **John 2:17**.

- Define the word 'passion.'

> **Then his disciples remembered this prophecy from the Scriptures: "Passion for God's house burns within me."**
>
> -John 2:17

- What will burn within Jesus?

- What can we learn about dealing with our anger from watching Jesus' actions in the temple?

- Do you think it is okay for us to become angry? Why?

your thoughts

_____
_____
_____
_____
_____
_____
_____
_____
_____
_____
_____
_____
_____

If you are true in character, you are able to combat any attack the Devil sends your way.

talk to God

_____
_____
_____
_____
_____
_____
_____
_____
_____
_____
_____
_____

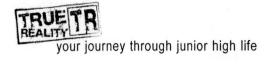
credits

- After completing this lesson, what are your thoughts on anger?

The credits section is designed to help you apply this week's chapter to your life. It can also be used for further discussion in a small group setting.

- What must you focus on in order to begin acting appropriately when you are angry?

- As Christians, should we ever let anger control us?

your thoughts

_____

_____

_____

_____

_____

_____

_____

_____

_____

_____

_____

_____

talk to God

The enemy desires that you think the task of sharing the Good News with others is a worthless and hopeless task.

_____

_____

_____

_____

_____

_____

_____

_____

_____

_____

_____

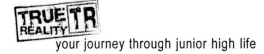

memory verse

- What are some key things to remember about being anger?

And "don't sin by letting anger gain control over you." Don't let the sun go down while you are still angry, for anger gives a mighty foothold to the Devil.

-Ephesians 4:26-27

- What is one thing I will commit to the Lord this week?

your thoughts

_____
_____
_____
_____
_____
_____
_____
_____
_____
_____
_____
_____

Only by memorizing God's Word are you able to use it as a sword in battle.

talk to God

_____
_____
_____
_____
_____
_____
_____
_____
_____
_____
_____

day seven

review

- What has God promised me this week?

keeping it real

Remember what God's word says about anger.

Take some time to answer these questions. It may not seem important now, but it will be awesome to look back and see how God has shaped your life.

- Does God have a command for me to obey?

- Have I done anything that I need forgiveness from God for?

- What lesson does God want me to remember this week?

- Questions about this study I need answered:

your thoughts

_____

_____

_____

_____

_____

_____

_____

_____

_____

_____

_____

_____

_____

If the devil can cause you to focus on your own selfish desires, he has won the battle.

talk to God

_____

_____

_____

_____

_____

_____

_____

_____

_____

_____

_____

_____

laziness

weekly verse

2 Thessalonians 3:10

Even while we were with you, we gave you this rule: "Whoever does not work should not eat."

trailer

Have you ever been accused of being lazy? If so, how did it make you feel? Did you care? Was your accuser right? I remember a situation where I was called lazy and it made me furious! I was in 8th grade and the fall semester was almost over. I was so excited because it was almost Christmas time and you know what that means…presents, presents, presents! I was at home hanging out with my family when I remembered I needed to get my parent's signature on a grade check report card for my classes. I pulled it out and showed it to both my mom and dad. They were irate! I began to see my dad's head turn red and my mom tried to calm him down. I guess they did have the right to get angry, though, because my grade check contained straight C's. I remember my dad looking into my eyes and telling me I had better pull my grades up, "or else." Then he spoke some words I will never forget, he said, "You can do way better than C's. I know you are not giving school your all. Turn things around and stop being so lazy." He said the magic word—lazy! I hate being called lazy, but in this instance my parents were right. I had become lazy with my schoolwork and I knew it. Over the course of an entire semester I had not done one ounce of work at home. I had fallen into the trap of laziness. Are you in that trap right now? Have you ever been in that trap?

preview

- When have you fallen into the trap of laziness? What happened?

first things first

Beginning with the end in mind helps you think through the purpose of what you want to learn before you actually learn it.

- Describe to your small group what an extremely lazy person looks and acts like.

- What do you think God's view on laziness is?

- Do you think that the world you live in is made up of hard workers or lazy people? Explain.

- Do you think God puts up with our laziness? Why/why not?

feature presentation

This week we are discussing what God's word says about laziness. It is so important that we understand God's perspective on this issue because the world we all live in is feeding us the counter truth. Our world tells us that it is okay to be late for appointments. It is okay to do the least amount of work required of us. Our culture says that it is okay not to give our best effort as long as the job gets completed. I don't know about you, but everyday I am tempted with laziness. It is the conviction of God's word that keeps me motivated to do my best in all I do. Ask God to reveal to you any areas of your life in which you have become lazy.

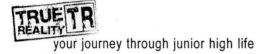

day one

Read **Proverbs 13:4.**

- Write the verse below.

Lazy people want much but
get little, but those who
work hard will prosper and
be satisfied.

-Proverbs 13:4

- What does it mean that the "those who work hard will prosper"?

- What will happen to the lazy man according to God's word?

- Does God ignore laziness? Why/why not?

your thoughts

_____
_____
_____
_____
_____
_____
_____
_____
_____
_____
_____
_____

As a Christian, you are called by God to stand out and be different from the rest of the world.

talk to God

_____
_____
_____
_____
_____
_____
_____
_____
_____
_____
_____
_____

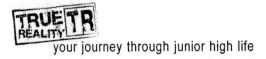
day two

Check out **Proverbs 19:15**.

- What does this verse say?

A lazy person sleeps soundly – and goes hungry.

-Proverbs 19:15

- What will laziness do to us?

- Is it wrong to sleep-in late? Why/why not?

- Who does God say will go hungry? Why will he go hungry?

your thoughts

_____

_____

_____

_____

_____

_____

_____

_____

_____

_____

_____

_____

_____

talk to God

If you are truly serious about making a difference in your world for Christ, you must first understand and practice true character.

_____

_____

_____

_____

_____

_____

_____

_____

_____

_____

_____

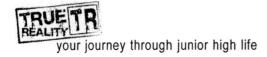
day three

Read **1 Thessalonians 5:12-14**.

- What's going on in these verses?

Dear brothers and sisters, honor those who are your leaders in the Lord's work. They work hard among you and warn you against all that is wrong. Think highly of them and give them your wholehearted love because of their work. And remember to live peaceably with each other. Brothers and sisters, we urge you to warn those who are lazy. Encourage those who are timid. Take tender care of those who are weak. Be patient with everyone.

-1 Thessalonians 5:12-14

- What do we gain if we work hard?

- Do you think respect is something each of us should strive and work for? Why/why not?

- In your own words, what do the last three sentences of this passage have to do with laziness?

_____
_____
_____
_____
_____
_____
_____
_____
_____
_____
_____
_____

God desires each Christian to know His Word and memorize it.

talk to God

_____
_____
_____
_____
_____
_____
_____
_____
_____
_____
_____
_____
_____

day four

Read **2 Thessalonians 3:10**.

- What is the significance of this verse?

Even while we were with you, we gave you this rule: "Whoever does not work should not eat."

-2 Thessalonians 3:10

- As God's children, what are we commanded to do?

- How can this verse be applied to you as a Junior High student? Explain.

your thoughts

_____
_____
_____
_____
_____
_____
_____
_____
_____
_____
_____
_____

The most difficult part of sharing your faith with your friends is asking them the first question about Jesus.

talk to God

_____
_____
_____
_____
_____
_____
_____
_____
_____
_____
_____

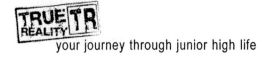

day five

credits

- After completing this lesson, how should a Christian view laziness?

The credits section is designed to help you apply this week's chapter to your life. It can also be used for further discussion in a small group setting.

- What must you do to begin to remove the laziness in your own life?

- Should we, as Christians, strive to be the laziest people possible? Explain.

- In your prayer time today, ask God to show you what you can be doing for Him! Then keep your eyes open for his answer to your prayer. God will open up ways for you to serve Him.

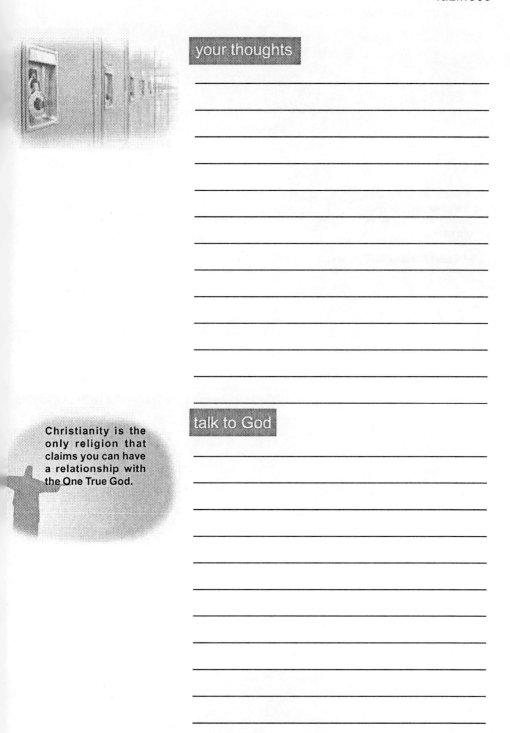

your thoughts

_____

_____

_____

_____

_____

_____

_____

_____

_____

_____

_____

talk to God

_____

_____

_____

_____

_____

_____

_____

_____

_____

_____

_____

Christianity is the only religion that claims you can have a relationship with the One True God.

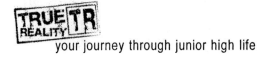
day six

memory verse

- Thinking back to what you've learned this week about laziness, what sticks out to you the most?

Even while we were with you, we gave you this rule: "Whoever does not work should not eat."

-2 Thessalonians 3:10

- What is one thing I will commit to the Lord this week?

your thoughts

_____
_____
_____
_____
_____
_____
_____
_____
_____
_____
_____
_____

talk to God

In order to know what is false, you must know and believe the truth about Jesus Christ and what He did for you on the cross.

_____
_____
_____
_____
_____
_____
_____
_____
_____
_____

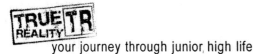
day seven

review

- What has God promised me this week?

keeping it real

With so many distractions in our world, it is difficult to keep from being lazy. Ask your small group leader for ideas of how to become less lazy, and dive in. There's no time to start like today. And I don't mean later today.

Take some time to answer these questions. It may not seem important now, but it will be awesome to look back and see how God has shaped your life.

- Does God have a command for me to obey?

- Have I done anything that I need forgiveness from God for?

- What lesson does God want me to remember this week?

- Questions about this study I need answered:

your thoughts

_____
_____
_____
_____
_____
_____
_____
_____
_____
_____
_____
_____
_____

God's desire is to see each Christian live a true life for Him.

talk to God

_____
_____
_____
_____
_____
_____
_____
_____
_____
_____
_____
_____
_____

pride

Proverbs 16:18

Pride goes before destruction, and
haughtiness before a fall.

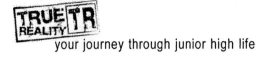
trailer

My senior year (12th grade) in high school I entered a guitar competition known as "Guitar Wars." For this competition I had to compose an original song and perform it live. I was so excited! Months past and I worked exceptionally hard. I spent long hours practicing so that my performance would be flawless. Finally, the day came when I was going to perform. I walked into a room filled with many people. There must have been five-hundred spectators there! I tuned my guitar up, then my name was called and I walked onto the stage to amaze the audience. I was filled with such joy, nervousness, and pride. I knew that I was good and I wanted everyone in the audience to know the same. I played my heart out with perfection. I received a standing ovation and I knew for sure I had placed. The time came to give out the awards. I sat with major anticipation as they read off the winners of 2nd and 3rd place. My name was not mentioned in either. I became restless. A brand new Ephiphone Les Paul Gold Top was awaiting first place winner. I couldn't wait. Finally the 1st place winner was announced. To my amazement I had been beat by a 12-year-old kid. I was totally bummed. I was almost certain that I had won. My ego was so big from my performance that I actually believed I was unbeatable. I had developed a huge case of pride. God shook me and woke me up that day saying, "Think again, you're not all that!" Looking back on that experience I learned a lot. I learned that pride does come before a fall and that I need to give God the praise and not myself.

preview

- When have you been filled with pride? What happened?

first things first

Beginning with the end in mind helps you think through the purpose of what you want to learn before you actually learn it.

- Have you ever lost something because your pride got in the way of reality?

- What do you think God's view on pride is?

feature presentation

This week we are discussing an issue each one of us deals with daily--pride. The Bible says that God despises the proud. God hates those people who are filled with pride and think that they don't need Him. Pride is a plague that has the potential to wipe us out if we do not keep it under control. Ask God to show you where your pride stems from. Then ask that He will show you how you may begin taking charge of your pride. We all have the potential to win the battle with pride. All we must do is ask God for help!

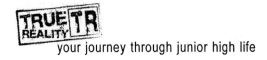

The memory verse is **Proverbs 16:18.**

- Write the verse below.

Pride goes before destruction, and haughtiness before a fall.

-Proverbs 16:18

- Define pride in your own words.

- Look up and write down the definition of haughtiness.

- Rewrite the verse in your own words.

- What does God think about pride?

your thoughts

_____

_____

_____

_____

_____

_____

_____

_____

_____

_____

_____

_____

If you are true in character, you are able to combat any attack the Devil sends your way.

talk to God

_____

_____

_____

_____

_____

_____

_____

_____

_____

_____

_____

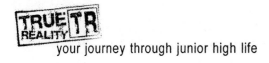

day two

Check out **Proverbs 29:23**.

- What does this verse say?

Pride ends in humiliation, while humility brings honor.

-Proverbs 29:23

- What will pride do to us?

- What does the verse mean, "humility brings honor"?

- If we are humble do we have to be quiet all the time and be pushovers?

- Would your friends consider you a person with pride or humility? Why?

your thoughts

_____

_____

_____

_____

_____

_____

_____

_____

_____

_____

_____

The enemy desires that you think the task of sharing the Good News with others is a worthless and hopeless task.

talk to God

_____

_____

_____

_____

_____

_____

_____

_____

_____

_____

_____

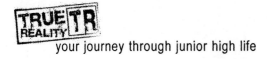

day three

Today's passage is **Jeremiah 50:31-32**.

- What's going on in these verses?

"See, I am your enemy, O proud people," says the Lord, the LORD Almighty. "Your day of reckoning has arrived. O land of pride, you will stumble and fall, and no one will raise you up. For I will light a fire in the cities of Babylon that will burn everything around them."

-Jeremiah 50:31-32

- What will happen to us if we are prideful? What does God declare?

- Does pride separate us from God?

your thoughts

_____

_____

_____

_____

_____

_____

_____

_____

_____

_____

_____

_____

_____

_____

Only by memorizing God's Word are you able to use it as a sword in battle.

talk to God

_____

_____

_____

_____

_____

_____

_____

_____

_____

_____

_____

_____

_____

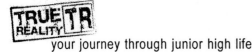
day four

Read **Ezekiel 16:48-50**.

• What happens to people who are prideful according to this passage?

As surely as I live, says the Sovereign LORD, Sodom and her daughters were never as wicked as you and your daughters. Sodom's sins were pride, laziness, and gluttony, while the poor and needy suffered outside her door. She was proud and did loathsome things, so I wiped her out, as you have seen.

-Ezekiel 16:48-50

• Where do evil thoughts, murder, adultery, sexual immorality, theft, false testimony, and slander come from?

Did you know? The city of Sodom was a symbol of total corruption. God completely destroyed the city because of its sin. Sodom was a city filled with sexual sins; however, Sodom was mainly destroyed because of the people's arrogance, gluttony, and unwillingness to help the poor. Sodom is being referred to here as a sister to Samaria—the capital of Israel. The Jews living in Judah didn't care about learning from Samaria and Sodom's previous mistakes. This meant that the people in Judah were of inevitable doom for the sins of Sodom.

• What does this passage mean when it says 'loathsome'?

your thoughts

_____

_____

_____

_____

_____

_____

_____

_____

_____

_____

_____

_____

_____

talk to God

If the devil can cause you to focus on your own selfish desires, he has won the battle.

_____

_____

_____

_____

_____

_____

_____

_____

_____

_____

_____

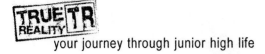
credits

- After completing this lesson, how would you describe pride?

The credits section is designed to help you apply this week's chapter to your life. It can also be used for further discussion in a small group setting.

- What must you focus on in order to begin developing true humility?

- How do you think people at your school will respond when you begin to become a more humble person?

- Write out a prayer asking God for Him to help you become a person of true humility.

your thoughts

talk to God

As a Christian, you are called by God to stand out and be different from the rest of the world.

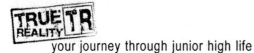
day six

memory verse

- What are some key things to remember about being truely humble?

Pride goes before destruction, and haughtiness before a fall.

-Proverbs 16:18

- What is one thing I will commit to the Lord this week?

your thoughts

_____
_____
_____
_____
_____
_____
_____
_____
_____
_____
_____
_____
_____
_____

If you are truly serious about making a difference in your world for Christ, you must first understand and practice true character.

talk to God

_____
_____
_____
_____
_____
_____
_____
_____
_____
_____
_____

day seven

review

- What has God promised me this week?

keeping it real

Pride not only destroys our relationship with God, it also hurts our relationships with our friends. Think about how many friends you have who act like they are better than you!

Take some time to answer these questions. It may not seem important now, but it will be awesome to look back and see how God has shaped your life.

- Does God have a command for me to obey?

- Have I done anything that I need forgiveness from God for?

- What lesson does God want me to remember this week?

- Questions about this study I need answered:

your thoughts

_____

_____

_____

_____

_____

_____

_____

_____

_____

_____

_____

God desires each Christian to know His Word and memorize it.

talk to God

_____

_____

_____

_____

_____

_____

_____

_____

_____

_____

_____

gossip

weekly verse

Proverbs 16:27-28

Scoundrels hunt for scandal; their words are a destructive blaze. A troublemaker plants seeds of strife; gossip separates the best of friends.

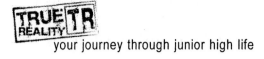
trailer

In this day and age TV is the main form of communication. Every show that is aired tries to persuade us to think a certain way, whether good or bad. You may be familiar with a show that went off the air a couple of years ago. It took situations, which were often absurd, that each person faced and dealt with them in a humorous way. This show was known as Seinfeld. If you have seen an episode of Seinfeld, you know that each character has major problems. They are all insecure, spastic, and lonely. The main characters, Jerry, George, Kramer, and Elaine are four single friends who share every distinct detail of their lives with each other. If you were to watch one episode, you would see that there is a large, complex gossip train ingrained within their dialogue. All four talk about themselves and others 24/7. Part of their humor is to make fun of others and what they are going through. Each character is constantly talking about other people. They describe what happens on the way to work, at work, lunch, on the way home, while at the movies, on a date, on the phone, with the postman, with ethnically diverse people, parents, and the like. This show is built upon gossip. The moral code that this show instills is weak. Gossip is a natural form of communication between each and every character. Gossip is always bad and is not a healthy way to communicate. How are you doing with gossip? Do you find yourself talking about others when they are not around? Do you make fun of other people behind their back? If so, you may have the Seinfeld problem of gossip.

preview

- Do you gossip? Why/why not?

first things first

Beginning with the end in mind helps you think through the purpose of what you want to learn before you actually learn it.

- Do you like people who gossip? Why/why not?

- What do you think God's view on gossip is?

feature presentation

This week we are discussing what God's word says about gossip. It is important to understand that God's word is clear about handling this issue. I believe that God is hurt when we as Christians hurt others; I don't mean just physically, but emotionally too. God is a loving God. He wants us to model our lives after His. If we are constantly putting others down, slamming them, and talking negatively about them behind their backs, how are we ever going to show them the love of God? Ask God to show you any areas in your life where gossip may be a problem. Pray that He will begin restoring relationships that you have damaged with your tongue.

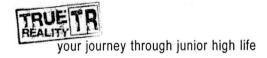
day one

Read **Exodus 23:1-2a.**

- How do these verses deal with gossip?

> **"Do not pass along false reports. Do not cooperate with evil people by telling lies on the witness stand. "Do not join a crowd that intends to do evil..."**
>
> -Exodus 23:1-2a

- Write this verse in your own words.

- When we gossip, do we follow the crowd? Are we doing it because it makes us look cool?

- In the long run, does your gossip (that is the gossip that you say) help or hurt you?

your thoughts

_____
_____
_____
_____
_____
_____
_____
_____
_____
_____
_____
_____
_____

The most difficult part of sharing your faith with your friends is asking them the first question about Jesus.

talk to God

_____
_____
_____
_____
_____
_____
_____
_____
_____
_____
_____

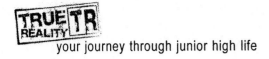
day two

Check out **Leviticus 19:16**.

- Write the verse here.

"Do not spread slanderous
gossip among your people.
"Do not try to get ahead at
the cost of your neighbor's
life, for I am the LORD..."

-Leviticus 19:16

- What is the difference between slanderous gossip and "regular" gossip?

- Why do you think God is so adamant about His people not talking badly about others?

- Write the verse here in your own words.

- How can you personally apply this verse at school today?

your thoughts

_____
_____
_____
_____
_____
_____
_____
_____
_____
_____
_____

Christianity is the only religion that claims you can have a relationship with the One True God.

talk to God

_____
_____
_____
_____
_____
_____
_____
_____
_____
_____
_____

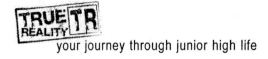

day three

Think about **Proverbs 16:27-28**.

- Who or what is a scoundrel?

Scoundrels hunt for scandal; their words are a destructive blaze. A troublemaker plants seeds of strife; gossip separates the best of friends.

-Proverbs 16:27-28

- Does God think gossip is perverse speech? Why/why not?

- Are we still at fault by listening to gossip, even if we do not actually spread it? Why/why not?

your thoughts

_____
_____
_____
_____
_____
_____
_____
_____
_____
_____
_____
_____

In order to know what is false, you must know and believe the truth about Jesus Christ and what He did for you on the cross.

talk to God

_____
_____
_____
_____
_____
_____
_____
_____
_____
_____
_____
_____

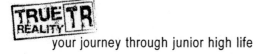

day four

Read **Proverbs 4:23-27**.

- What do these verses say for us to do?

> Above all else, guard your heart, for it affects everything you do. Avoid all perverse talk; stay far from corrupt speech. Look straight ahead, and fix your eyes on what lies before you. Mark out a straight path for your feet; then stick to the path and stay safe. Don't get sidetracked; keep your feet from following evil.
>
> -Proverbs 4:23-27

- What happens if our eyes are focused straight ahead on God?

- What does it mean to "mark out a straight path for your feet"?

- Are we entering into an evil act if we gossip? Why/why not?

your thoughts

_____
_____
_____
_____
_____
_____
_____
_____
_____
_____
_____
_____

God's desire is to see each Christian live a true life for Him.

talk to God

_____
_____
_____
_____
_____
_____
_____
_____
_____
_____
_____

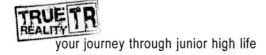
credits

- What does God's word say about Christians and gossip?

The credits section is designed to help you apply this week's chapter to your life. It can also be used for further discussion in a small group setting.

- What must you focus on in order to get rid of gossip in your life?

- What do you think we, as Christians, should do if we find ourselves caught in the trap of gossip?

- List some ways the habit of gossip can be overcome?

your thoughts

_____

_____

_____

_____

_____

_____

_____

_____

_____

_____

_____

_____

If you are true in character, you are able to combat any attack the Devil sends your way.

talk to God

_____

_____

_____

_____

_____

_____

_____

_____

_____

_____

_____

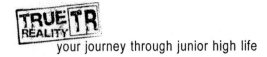
day six

memory verse

- What do you remember about gossip?

Scoundrels hunt for scandal; their words are a destructive blaze. A troublemaker plants seeds of strife; gossip separates the best of friends.

-Proverbs 16:27-28

- What is one thing I will commit to the Lord this week?

CCS

your thoughts

_____

_____

_____

_____

_____

_____

_____

_____

_____

_____

_____

talk to God

The enemy desires that you think the task of sharing the Good News with others is a worthless and hopeless task.

_____

_____

_____

_____

_____

_____

_____

_____

_____

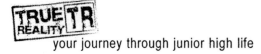

day seven

review

- What has God promised me this week?

keeping it real

Gossip can be a devastating trap to be involved in. It can destroy friendships and create conflict between yourself and others.

Take some time to answer these questions. It may not seem important now, but it will be awesome to look back and see how God has shaped your life.

- Does God have a command for me to obey?

- Have I done anything that I need forgiveness from God for?

- What lesson does God want me to remember this week?

- Questions about this study I need answered:

_____
_____
_____
_____
_____
_____
_____
_____
_____
_____
_____
_____

Only by memorizing God's Word are you able to use it as a sword in battle.

talk to God

_____
_____
_____
_____
_____
_____
_____
_____
_____
_____
_____
_____
_____

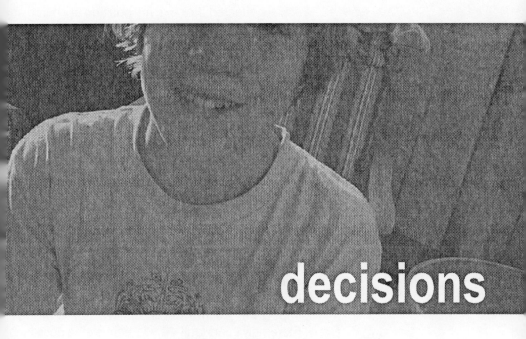

decisions

weekly verse

Psalm 119:105-106

Your word is a lamp for my feet and a light for my
path. I've promised it once, and I'll promise again:
I will obey your wonderful laws.

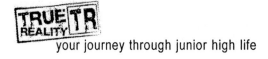
trailer

Everyday each one of us is faced with decisions. Some decisions we make are good and some are bad. For many people, decision making is a very hard process. This is primarily because when we make decisions someone or something else is always affected. For me, my position at church as a Pastor puts me into a high profile role. What that means is that every decision I make will in someway be heard, found out, or affect each person under my leadership. I am forced to decide how I am going to make decisions daily. I wake up in the morning and the first decision I make is to spend time with God. I do my devotions because I know that without God's input, my decisions will be worthless. The second decision I make is to spend time in prayer. I want to dialogue with God. I want Him to input into my life. The third decision I make is to look to Him throughout the day for answers to difficult decisions. When a problem arises, I take it to God. He is faithful and every time He gives me some answer as to what I should do. The most important decision I make daily is to live for God. Without Christ's input into our lives, we most certainly will screw up. How important are the decisions we make in life? Extremely important! Why? Because the decisions that each of us make daily will directly affect our attitudes, and people look at our attitudes to see what kind of character we have. Decision making is an extremely important task that each of us practices daily.

preview

- Is it easy for you to make decisions? Why/why not?

first things first

Beginning with the end in mind helps you think through the purpose of what you want to learn before you actually learn it.

- Are you someone who looks to God first when forced to make a decision? Explain.

- Are the decisions you make daily generally good or bad? Explain.

- What is the worst decision you have ever made?

feature presentation

This week we are looking at how we make true decisions. We must understand that God desires to help us with our decision making. Scripture is filled with many leaders who were forced into difficult situations where they had to make decisions that not only affected themselves but thousands of other people. For instance, Moses had multiple decisions when exiting God's people out of Egypt. King Saul had a huge decision when David asked to fight Goliath. The point is, even the biggest and baddest Bible characters had to choose whether or not they would turn to God when crisis arose. Are you an true decision maker? Do you turn to God during crisis, or do you try and do it on your own? Ask God to open your heart, mind, and soul as we begin our study on true decisions.

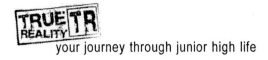

day one

Read **Psalm 119:105-106.**

- What does this passage say guides our path in life?

Your word is a lamp for my feet and a light for my path. I've promised it once, and I'll promise again: I will obey your wonderful laws.

-Psalm 119:105-106

- What does it mean, "Your word is a lamp for my feet and a light for my path"?

- Have you put your faith in Jesus?

  If you have not and would like to, call your small group leader or another Christian role model in your life right now. If you do not have one, call toll-free 1-888-NEED-HIM. Someone is waiting to speak with you now.

- If you have, does that count as a promise to follow God's rules? Why/why not?

your thoughts

_____

_____

_____

_____

_____

_____

_____

_____

_____

_____

_____

If the devil can cause you to focus on your own selfish desires, he has won the battle.

talk to God

_____

_____

_____

_____

_____

_____

_____

_____

_____

_____

_____

_____

day two

Check out **Ezekiel 11:12**.

- What does this passage say?

"..and you will know that I am the LORD. For you have refused to obey me; instead, you have copied the sins of the nations around you."

-Ezekiel 11:12

- From this passage who did Israel follow?

Did you know? From the time that the Israelites entered the promise land, they were warned not to copy the religious practices and customs of the other nations. Disobeying God and making poor decisions always got them into trouble. Today, we as believers are tempted daily, just like the Israelites, to fall into the ways of the world. We must get our standards of right and wrong from God, not from the popular trends of magazines and TV.

- According to this passage, did Israel make a good choice of who they would follow? Why?

- Do you imitate God while you are at school? Why/why not?

your thoughts

_____

_____

_____

_____

_____

_____

_____

_____

_____

_____

_____

_____

_____

As a Christian, you are called by God to stand out and be different from the rest of the world.

talk to God

_____

_____

_____

_____

_____

_____

_____

_____

_____

_____

_____

_____

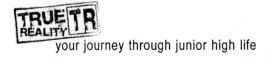
day three

Take a look at **Judges 6:1**.

- What in the world does this verse mean?

Again the Israelites did what was evil in the LORD's sight. So the LORD handed them over to the Midianites for seven years.

-Judges 6:1

- If our decisions always go against what God wants, is He going to bless us? Why/why not?

- What happened to the Israelites when they decided not to obey and worship God?

- Have you disobeyed God this week by making poor decisions? What were they? Why?

your thoughts

_____

_____

_____

_____

_____

_____

_____

_____

_____

_____

_____

_____

talk to God

If you are truly serious about making a difference in your world for Christ, you must first understand and practice true character.

_____

_____

_____

_____

_____

_____

_____

_____

_____

_____

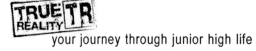
day four

Read **Matthew 7:1-5**.

- What do these verses have to say about decision making?

"Stop judging others, and you will not be judged. For others will treat you as you treat them. Whatever measure you use in judging others, it will be used to measure how you are judged. And why worry about a speck in your friend's eye when you have a log in your own? How can you think of saying, 'Let me help you get rid of that speck in your eye,' when you can't see past the log in your own eye? Hypocrite! First get rid of the log from your own eye; then perhaps you will see well enough to deal with the speck in your friend's eye.

-Matthew 7:1-5

- If we are critical and judgmental of others, how does that affect the decisions we make toward them?

- What does God say about judging others?

- Have you made poor decisions because you were critical or judgmental of others? What were they? What happened?

- If our decisions always go against what God wants, is He going to bless us? Why/why not?

- Have you disobeyed God this week by making poor decisions? What were they? Why?

your thoughts

_____
_____
_____
_____
_____
_____
_____
_____
_____
_____
_____
_____

God desires each Christian to know His Word and memorize it.

talk to God

_____
_____
_____
_____
_____
_____
_____
_____
_____
_____
_____

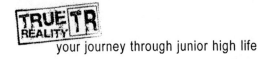
credits

- What does God's word say about how we should make true decisions?

- What must you focus on in order to make true decisions?

The credits section is designed to help you apply this week's chapter to your life. It can also be used for further discussion in a small group setting.

- How do you become a true decision maker?

- List some steps to help you make better decisions.

your thoughts

_____
_____
_____
_____
_____
_____
_____
_____
_____
_____
_____

The most difficult part of sharing your faith with your friends is asking them the first question about Jesus.

talk to God

_____
_____
_____
_____
_____
_____
_____
_____
_____
_____
_____

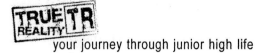

day six

memory verse

- What are some key things to remember about being a true decision maker?

Your word is a lamp for my feet and a light for my path. I've promised it once, and I'll promise again: I will obey your wonderful laws.

-Psalm 119:105-106

- What is one thing I will commit to the Lord this week?

your thoughts

_____
_____
_____
_____
_____
_____
_____
_____
_____
_____
_____
_____

Christianity is the only religion that claims you can have a relationship with the One True God.

talk to God

_____
_____
_____
_____
_____
_____
_____
_____
_____
_____
_____

day seven

review

- What has God promised me this week?

keeping it real

Making true decisions is extremely important. Making one bad decision can mess up the rest of your life!

Take some time to answer these questions. It may not seem important now, but it will be awesome to look back and see how God has shaped your life.

- Does God have a command for me to obey?

- Have I done anything that I need forgiveness from God for?

- What lesson does God want me to remember this week?

- Questions about this study I need answered:

your thoughts

_____

_____

_____

_____

_____

_____

_____

_____

_____

_____

_____

_____

talk to God

In order to know what is false, you must know and believe the truth about Jesus Christ and what He did for you on the cross.

_____

_____

_____

_____

_____

_____

_____

_____

_____

_____

_____

_____

courage

weekly verse

Joshua 1:9

I command you – be strong and courageous! Do not be afraid or discouraged. For the LORD your God is with you wherever you go."

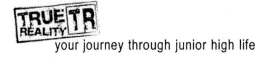
trailer

Have you ever been rock climbing? If not, you're missing out! Rock climbing is one of my all time favorite sports. I love climbing. This love for climbing started back when I was fifteen years old. My small group leader was really into climbing, so I asked him if he would teach me. He said, "Sure!" My leader and I went up to a rock known as Tollhouse Rock. This is a monstrous rock standing hundreds of feet above the ground. As we hiked to the base of this rock I kept looking at the height of the rock and was filled with fear. You see, I had never climbed before and the thought of falling hundreds of feet to my death did not appeal to me. I began to share with my leader my concerns about the climb. I told him that I was scared and wasn't sure that I was up for it. I can vividly remember what he told me next. He said, "You know, I realize it looks scary, but, when you reach the top you will have accomplished something most people will never accomplish in their lifetime. The only thing that stands between you and success is courage! My leader's talk pumped me up. I was ready to go the distance. I climbed the rock and reached the top safely. I was never more stoked than looking down only to see how far I had come. That is one day I will always remember. That day on the rock I was filled with true courage.

preview

- Do you have a problem with a lack of courage?

first things first

Beginning with the end in mind helps you think through the purpose of what you want to learn before you actually learn it.

- Have you ever been too scared to do something? What was it? What happened?

- How does God fill His children with courage?

- Do you think it is okay to be scared? Why/why not?

- What does true courage mean to you?

feature presentation

This week we are discussing true courage. Living sold-out lives for Christ is not easy. In fact, many times in the Bible Paul writes for Christ's followers to have the courage to endure the hardships that lie ahead of them. Living for Christ can be scary. Sharing our faith with our friends is scary. However, the one thing that separates active Christians from inactive Christians is true courage. Ask God to build your courage this week. Tell God that you want to be an active Christian—totally sold-out for Christ!

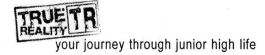

day one

Read **Joshua 1:9** & **Isaiah 12:2.**

- What gave Joshua courage during battle?

I command you – be strong and courageous! Do not be afraid or discouraged. For the LORD your God is with you wherever you go."

-Joshua 1:9

See, God has come to save me. I will trust in him and not be afraid. The LORD GOD is my strength and my song; he has become my salvation."

-Isaiah 12:2

- Would people say you are a Joshua? Why/why not?

Did you know? Joshua was a brilliant military officer who was chosen to lead the people of Israel to conquer the promise land (Canaan) after Moses' death. Joshua was a man who obeyed God. His obedience is what gave him the courage to stand up to the many enemies he was forced to face. In the end, however, God blessed him and the people of Israel prospered.

- Why should we not be afraid of hardships?

your thoughts

_____

_____

_____

_____

_____

_____

_____

_____

_____

_____

_____

_____

_____

God's desire is to see each Christian live a true life for Him.

talk to God

_____

_____

_____

_____

_____

_____

_____

_____

_____

_____

_____

_____

day two

Check out **Haggai 2:4**.

- What does this scripture say?

But now take courage, Zerubbabel, says the LORD. Take courage, Jeshua son of Jehozadak, the high priest. Take courage, all you people still left in the land, says the LORD. Take courage and work, for I am with you, says the LORD Almighty.

-Haggai 2:4

- Why does God tell the people of Judah to work?

Did you know? Judah's people had returned to worshiping God, and God had promised to bless their efforts. However, the time of prayer, Bible study, and worship had overtaken their work and God wanted them to get off their rears and change things for His kingdom. That is why God told them to, "Be strong...and work. For I am with you." God wants us to spend time in prayer, Bible study, and worship, but when it overtakes our willingness to be used to further God's kingdom God says "work." In order to "work" for God we must have "courage."

- What is the significance of work?

- Are you so caught up in the "Barbie" Christian life that you're too scared to work for God? Why/ why not?

_____

_____

_____

_____

_____

_____

_____

_____

_____

_____

_____

_____

If you are true in character, you are able to combat any attack the Devil sends your way.

talk to God

_____

_____

_____

_____

_____

_____

_____

_____

_____

_____

_____

_____

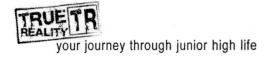
day three

Read **Acts 4:13** & **1 Corinthians 16:13**.

- Why was the council that Peter and John stood before so amazed?

The members of the council were amazed when they saw the boldness of Peter and John, for they could see that they were ordinary men who had had no special training. They also recognized them as men who had been with Jesus.

-Acts 4:13

- What is more powerful: A person of great Biblical knowledge or a person with a changed life living sold-out for Christ? Why?

Be on guard. Stand true to what you believe. Be courageous. Be strong.

-1 Corinthians 16:13

- What do we all need in order to be people with true courage?

_____

_____

_____

_____

_____

_____

_____

_____

_____

_____

_____

If you are true in character, you are able to combat any attack the Devil sends your way.

talk to God

_____

_____

_____

_____

_____

_____

_____

_____

_____

_____

_____

_____

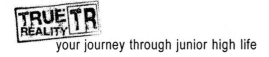
day four

Read **Philippians 1:20-21**.

- What do these verses have to say?

For I live in eager expectation and hope that I will never do anything that causes me shame, but that I will always be bold for Christ, as I have been in the past, and that my life will always honor Christ, whether I live or I die. For to me, living is for Christ, and dying is even better.

-Philippians 1:20-21

- Why does Paul want courage?

- What would Paul be ashamed of if he didn't gain enough courage?

- Rewrite the second half in your own words. Why is this verse so cool?

- Is Paul willing to die being courageous for Christ's sake? Why?

your thoughts

_____
_____
_____
_____
_____
_____
_____
_____
_____
_____
_____
_____
_____

The enemy desires that you think the task of sharing the Good News with others is a worthless and hopeless task.

talk to God

_____
_____
_____
_____
_____
_____
_____
_____
_____
_____
_____
_____

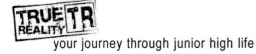
credits

- After completing this lesson, what does true courage look like to you?

The credits section is designed to help you apply this week's chapter to your life. It can also be used for further discussion in a small group setting.

- What must you focus on in order to begin developing true courage for God?

- If all Christians strived for the same amount of courage as Paul, do you think we all would impact our cities in a greater way? Why/why not?

- In your daily prayer, ask God for Him to help you become a person of true courage.

your thoughts

_____
_____
_____
_____
_____
_____
_____
_____
_____
_____
_____
_____
_____

Only by memorizing God's Word are you able to use it as a sword in battle.

talk to God

_____
_____
_____
_____
_____
_____
_____
_____
_____
_____
_____

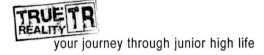

your journey through junior high life

day six

memory verse

- What do you remember about true courage?

I command you – be strong
and courageous! Do not be
afraid or discouraged. For
the LORD your God is with
you wherever you go."

-Joshua 1:9

- What is one thing I will commit to the Lord this week?

your thoughts

_____
_____
_____
_____
_____
_____
_____
_____
_____
_____
_____
_____
_____
_____

talk to God

If the devil can cause you to focus on your own selfish desires, he has won the battle.

_____
_____
_____
_____
_____
_____
_____
_____
_____
_____
_____
_____

day seven

review

- What has God promised me this week?

keeping it real

Have true courage! Do not be timid about the things of God. Boldly tell others about what He has done in your life and what Christ can do for them.

Take some time to answer these questions. It may not seem important now, but it will be awesome to look back and see how God has shaped your life.

- Does God have a command for me to obey?

- Have I done anything that I need forgiveness from God for?

- What lesson does God want me to remember this week?

- Questions about this study I need answered:

_____

_____

_____

_____

_____

_____

_____

_____

_____

_____

_____

_____

_____

As a Christian, you are called by God to stand out and be different from the rest of the world.

talk to God

_____

_____

_____

_____

_____

_____

_____

_____

_____

_____

_____

_____

_____

friendship

weekly verse

John 15:13

And here is how to measure it – the greatest love is shown when people lay down their lives for their friends.

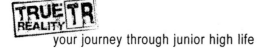
trailer

Have you ever had a friend that you know would, without a doubt, die for you? In this day and age true friendship is enormously hard to find. I have had many people in my life that I've called friends, but realistically I have only had three true friends. These three friends have stood by me through my stupid times, sad times, and challenging times when I felt alone and confused. All three have in some giant way contributed to the making of who I am. However, as I think of the term true friendship, I recognize that two things can happen. First, you can pick the wrong group of friends, which can cost you more than you're willing to give. Second, you can pick friends who encourage and push you towards greatness, and you will loose nothing. The saying, "you can pick your friend's, you can pick your nose, but can't pick your friends nose" is so true. We all have in our power who we choose to call friends and hang with. We also can choose to pick our nose if we want; however, the part about us not being able to pick our friends nose is ultimately true. Although technically we can pick our friend's nose (you'd have to be an extremely sick person) what this saying means is that we cannot make our friend's decisions for them. In each situation we encounter, we either choose to do right or wrong. And although we can influence our friends to do the same, we cannot choose for them.

preview

- What is true friendship mean to you?

first things first

Beginning with the end in mind helps you think through the purpose of what you want to learn before you actually learn it.

- Would any of your friends lay their life down to save yours? Who are they?

- List the people you are thinking about hanging out with this year at school.

- What kind of influence do they have on you? Be honest.

feature presentation

This week we are going to look at two friends from the Bible who had true friendship. They are Jonathan and David. Through observing the lives of these two guys in scripture we will see how God intends for our friendships to operate. As we begin the semester this year we want to develop true friendships and influence others towards God, not be influenced from others to turn from God. Before you begin, ask God to open your heart and show you any relationship you need to work on.

day one

Read **1 Samuel 18:1-9.**

- What happens in this passage?

After David had finished talking with Saul, he met Jonathan, the king's son. There was an immediate bond of love between them, and they became the best of friends. From that day on Saul kept David with him at the palace and wouldn't let him return home. And Jonathan made a special vow to be David's friend, and he sealed the pact by giving him his robe, tunic, sword, bow, and belt. Whatever Saul asked David to do, David did it successfully. So Saul made him a commander in his army, an appointment that was applauded by the fighting men and officers alike. But something happened when the victorious Israelite army was returning home after David had killed Goliath. Women came out from all the towns along the way to celebrate and to cheer for King Saul, and they sang and danced for joy with tambourines and cymbals. This was their song: "Saul has killed his thousands, and David his ten thousands!" This made Saul very angry. "What's this?" he said. "They credit David with ten thousands and me with only thousands. Next they'll be making him their king!" So from that time on Saul kept a jealous eye on David.

-1 Samuel 18:1-9

- What did Jonathan immediately do when he first met David?

- From this passage, would you say Jonathan has a true friendship with David (look at the beginning)? Why/why not?

- Why do you think Jonathan does not become jealous of David like his father does?

your thoughts

_____

_____

_____

_____

_____

_____

_____

_____

_____

_____

_____

talk to God

If you are truly serious about making a difference in your world for Christ, you must first understand and practice true character.

_____

_____

_____

_____

_____

_____

_____

_____

_____

_____

Saul now urged his servants and his son Jonathan to assassinate David. But Jonathan, because of his close friendship with David, told him what his father was planning. "Tomorrow morning," he warned him, "you must find a hiding place out in the fields. I'll ask my father to go out there with me, and I'll talk to him about you. Then I'll tell you everything I can find out." The next morning Jonathan spoke with his father about David, saying many good things about him. "Please don't sin against David," Jonathan pleaded. "He's never done anything to harm you. He has always helped you in any way he could. Have you forgotten about the time he risked his life to kill the Philistine giant and how the LORD brought a great victory to Israel as a result? You were certainly happy about it then. Why should you murder an innocent man like David? There is no reason for it at all!" So Saul listened to Jonathan and vowed, "As surely as the LORD lives, David will not be killed." Afterward Jonathan called David and told him what had happened. Then he took David to see Saul, and everything was as it had been before. War broke out shortly after that, and David led his troops against the Philistines. He attacked them with such fury that they all ran away. But one day as Saul was sitting at home, the tormenting spirit from the LORD suddenly came upon him again. As David played his harp for the king,

-1 Samuel 19:1-9

Check out **1 Samuel 19:1-9**.

- Why is Saul trying to kill David?

- What does Jonathan do?

- In the face of danger, why does Jonathan risk his life and stand up for David?

- What happens after Saul agrees not to harm David?

- Are true friendships based on jealousy or trust? What happens when we become jealous of our friends?

your thoughts

_____

_____

_____

_____

_____

_____

_____

_____

_____

_____

_____

talk to God

God desires each Christian to know His Word and memorize it.

_____

_____

_____

_____

_____

_____

_____

_____

_____

_____

_____

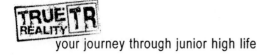
day three

Read **1 Samuel 20:1-4**.

- What does David tell Jonathan?

- Does Jonathan believe David?

- What is Jonathan's response to David?

- Do you have a friend who would respond to you like Jonathan does to David if you were in trouble?

- Is Jonathan more concerned about himself or his friend David?

- Are the people you call friends often more concerned with your well-being or their own?

David now fled from Naioth in Ramah and found Jonathan. "What have I done?" he exclaimed. "What is my crime? How have I offended your father that he is so determined to kill me?" "That's not true!" Jonathan protested. "I'm sure he's not planning any such thing, for he always tells me everything he's going to do, even the little things. I know he wouldn't hide something like this from me. It just isn't so!" Then David took an oath before Jonathan and said, "Your father knows perfectly well about our friendship, so he has said to himself, 'I won't tell Jonathan — why should I hurt him?' But I swear to you that I am only a step away from death! I swear it by the LORD and by your own soul!" "Tell me what I can do!" Jonathan exclaimed.

-1 Samuel 20:1-4

your thoughts

_____
_____
_____
_____
_____
_____
_____
_____
_____
_____
_____
_____
_____

The most difficult part of sharing your faith with your friends is asking them the first question about Jesus.

talk to God

_____
_____
_____
_____
_____
_____
_____
_____
_____
_____
_____
_____

So Jonathan made a covenant with David, saying, "May the LORD destroy all your enemies!" And Jonathan made David reaffirm his vow of friendship again, for Jonathan loved David as much as he loved himself. Then Jonathan said, "Tomorrow we celebrate the new moon festival. You will be missed when your place at the table is empty. The day after tomorrow, toward evening, go to the place where you hid before, and wait there by the stone pile. I will come out and shoot three arrows to the side of the stone pile as though I were shooting at a target. Then I will send a boy to bring the arrows back. If you hear me tell him, 'They're on this side,' then you will know, as surely as the LORD lives, that all is well, and there is no trouble. But if I tell him, 'Go farther – the arrows are still ahead of you,' then it will mean that you must leave immediately, for the LORD is sending you away. And may the LORD make us keep our promises to each other, for he has witnessed them." So David hid himself in the field, and when the new moon festival began, the king sat down to eat. He sat at his usual place against the wall, with Jonathan sitting opposite him and Abner beside him. But David's place was empty. Saul didn't say anything about it that day, for he said to himself, "Something must have made David ceremonially unclean. Yes, that must be why he's not here." But when David's place was empty again the next day, Saul asked Jonathan, "Why hasn't the son of Jesse been here for dinner either yesterday or today?" Jonathan replied, "David earnestly asked me if he could go to Bethlehem. He wanted to take part in a family sacrifice. His brother demanded that he be there, so I told him he could go. That's why he isn't

day four

Read **1 Samuel 20:16-42**.

- What happens in these verses?

- In the first verse, what does Jonathan reaffirm to David? Why does he do this?

- What happens when David doesn't show up to the banquet?

- What happens after Jonathan signals David with his arrows?

- Why is Jonathan such a true friend to David?

ere." Saul boiled with rage at Jonathan. "You stupid son of a whore!" he swore at him. "Do you think I don't know that you want David to be king in your place, shaming yourself and your mother? As long as that son of Jesse is alive, you'll never be king. Now go and get him so I can kill him!" "But what has he done?" Jonathan demanded. "Why should he be put to death?" Then Saul hurled his spear at Jonathan, intending to kill him. So at last Jonathan realized that his father was really determined to kill David. Jonathan left the table in fierce anger and refused to eat all that day, for he was crushed by his father's shameful behavior toward David. The next morning, as agreed, Jonathan went out into the field and took a young boy with him to gather his arrows. "Start running," he told the boy, "so you can find the arrows as I shoot them." So the boy ran, and Jonathan shot an arrow beyond him. When the boy had almost reached the arrow, Jonathan shouted, "The arrow is still ahead of you. Hurry, hurry, don't wait." So the boy quickly gathered up the arrows and ran back to his master. He, of course, didn't understand what Jonathan meant; only Jonathan and David knew. Then Jonathan gave his bow and arrows to the boy and told him to take them back to the city. As soon as the boy was gone, David came out from where he had been hiding near the stone pile. Then David bowed to Jonathan with his face to the ground. Both of them were in tears as they embraced each other and said good-bye, especially David. At last Jonathan said to David, "Go in peace, for we have made a pact in the LORD's name. We have entrusted each other and each other's children into the LORD's hands forever." Then David left, and Jonathan returned to the city.

-1 Samuel 20:16-42

your thoughts

talk to God

199

day five

credits

- After completing this lesson, what does true friendship look like to you now?

The credits section is designed to help you apply this week's chapter to your life. It can also be used for further discussion in a small group setting.

- Are you a "Jonathan" to the friends you hang around?

- Why are truthful, loyal, true friends so important to have?

- Are the people you call friends more concerned with your well-being or their own?

your thoughts

_____
_____
_____
_____
_____
_____
_____
_____
_____
_____
_____
_____

talk to God

Christianity is the only religion that claims you can have a relationship with the One True God.

_____
_____
_____
_____
_____
_____
_____
_____
_____
_____
_____

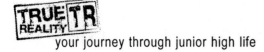

day six

memory verse

- What are some key things to remember about having and being true friends?

And here is how to measure it – the greatest love is shown when people lay down their lives for their friends.

-John 15:13

- What is one thing I will commit to the Lord this week?

your thoughts

_____

_____

_____

_____

_____

_____

_____

_____

_____

_____

_____

_____

In order to know
what is false, you
must know and
believe the truth
about Jesus Christ
and what He did for
you on the cross.

talk to God

_____

_____

_____

_____

_____

_____

_____

_____

_____

_____

_____

keeping it real

True friendship is ultimately important to your true reality.

Take some time to answer these questions. It may not seem important now, but it will be awesome to look back and see how God has shaped your life.

day seven

review

- What has God promised me this week?

- Does God have a command for me to obey?

- Have I done anything that I need forgiveness from God for?

- What lesson does God want me to remember this week?

- Questions about this study I need answered:

your thoughts

_____
_____
_____
_____
_____
_____
_____
_____
_____
_____
_____

God's desire is to
see each Christian
live a true life for Him.

talk to God

_____
_____
_____
_____
_____
_____
_____
_____
_____
_____
_____
_____
_____

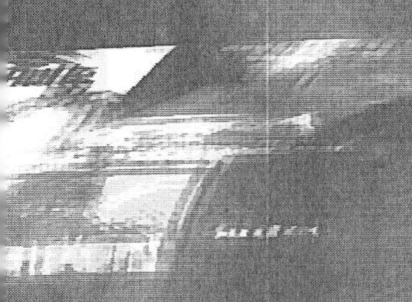

character

Titus 1:7

An elder must live a blameless life because he
is God's minister. He must not be arrogant or
quick-tempered; he must not be a heavy drinker,
violent, or greedy for money.

trailer

Have you ever thought about what the term character means? I have! In fact, each and every day when I wake up, the first thing that goes through my mind is that I need to have an unquestionable character. So what is character anyway? Webster defines character as "the moral or ethical structure of a person." To make it a bit easier to understand, character is what people talk about when they are telling other people what you are like. For example, your friend might be talking about their teacher and he/she says, "Mr. _____ is such a jerk. He is always telling us one thing and doing another. He told us that the questions in our homework assignment were not going to be on the test so the class didn't do the work, when actually the test was made specifically from our homework questions. What a liar! Don't ever take one of his classes; he can't be trusted." Your friend, without knowing it, was attacking their teacher's character. To have true character is what each of us as Christians should strive for. We need to be above reproach (that means we need to be above the world's standards). If we strive to achieve a true character, our friends can not help but be introduced to our living God!

preview

- What does having an true character mean to you?

- How would your friends describe you?

- How would your teachers describe you?

- If your Pastor were to go onto your school campus and watch you without you knowing, would your character show Christ? Why/why not?

- How can you begin to develop a true character like God's?

first things first

Beginning with the end in mind helps you think through the purpose of what you want to learn before you actually learn it.

feature presentation

You guessed it, this week we are going to be looking at how we as Christians can develop a true character for Christ. We are going to flip through scripture and look at what each of us needs to have in order to maintain a true character. Before we begin, stop and ask God to reveal to you what you are really like. Ask Him to show you what your true character is right now. Then ask Him to help guide you through the study this week as you learn and apply these things to develop a true character for Him.

day one

Take a look at **Job 1:1.**

- According to this verse, what kind of man is Job?

There was a man named Job who lived in the land of Uz. He was blameless, a man of complete integrity. He feared God and stayed away from evil.

-Job 1:1

- What does it mean to be blameless?

Did you know? Job lost all he had no fault of his own. As he struggled to understand why all this was happening to him, it became clear that God was testing his character. By not knowing the why's to his life, he was able to develop his faith in God fully. Job was a man of true character. (Check his story out, it's a long book, but worth the read).

- Why must we fear God in order to have a true character? What does it mean to fear God?

your thoughts

_____

_____

_____

_____

_____

_____

_____

_____

_____

_____

_____

_____

If you are true in character, you are able to combat any attack the Devil sends your way.

talk to God

_____

_____

_____

_____

_____

_____

_____

_____

_____

_____

_____

_____

day two

Check out **Jeremiah 7:5-11**.

- What in the world is this passage talking about?

I will be merciful only if you stop your wicked thoughts and deeds and are fair to others; and if you stop exploiting foreigners, orphans, and widows; and if you stop your murdering; and if you stop worshiping idols as you now do to your own harm. Then I will let you stay in this land that I gave to your ancestors to keep forever."'Do you think that because the Temple is here you will never suffer? Don't fool yourselves! Do you really think you can steal, murder, commit adultery, lie, and worship Baal and all those other new gods of yours, and then come here and stand before me in my Temple and chant, "We are safe!" – only to go right back to all those evils again? Do you think this Temple, which honors my name, is a den of thieves? I see all the evil going on there, says the LORD.

-Jeremiah 7:5-11

- What does the end of this passage mean when it asks, "Do you think this Temple, which honors my name, is a den of thieves"?

- Do you believe that God watches your actions all day, every day? Does it matter to God that you act one way at school, another at home, and yet another way at church? Why/why not?

your thoughts

_____
_____
_____
_____
_____
_____
_____
_____
_____
_____
_____
_____

The enemy desires that you think the task of sharing the Good News with others is a worthless and hopeless task.

talk to God

_____
_____
_____
_____
_____
_____
_____
_____
_____
_____
_____
_____

day three

Read **Ezekiel 3:4-9.**

- What happens in this passage?

I will be merciful only if you stop your wicked thoughts and deeds and are fair to others; and if you stop exploiting foreigners, orphans, and widows; and if you stop your murdering; and if you stop worshiping idols as you now do to your own harm. Then I will let you stay in this land that I gave to your ancestors to keep forever.'"Do you think that because the Temple is here you will never suffer? Don't fool yourselves! Do you really think you can steal, murder, commit adultery, lie, and worship Baal and all those other new gods of yours, and then come here and stand before me in my Temple and chant, "We are safe!" – only to go right back to all those evils again? Do you think this Temple, which honors my name, is a den of thieves? I see all the evil going on there, says the LORD.

-Ezekiel 3:4-9

- Why do you think Ezekiel is unwilling to listen to God?

- What does God promise Ezekiel? What is He going to do to his forehead?

- What does the end of this passage mean?

- Do you listen to God? Does your character possess stubbornness for God? Why/why not?

your thoughts

_____

_____

_____

_____

_____

_____

_____

_____

_____

_____

_____

_____

Only by memorizing God's Word are you able to use it as a sword in battle.

talk to God

_____

_____

_____

_____

_____

_____

_____

_____

_____

_____

_____

_____

_____

day four

Read **Titus 1:7-9**.

- What does a true character look like?

Then he said, "Son of man, go to the people of Israel with my messages. I am not sending you to some foreign people whose language you cannot understand. No, I am not sending you to people with strange and difficult speech. If I did, they would listen! I am sending you to the people of Israel, but they won't listen to you any more than they listen to me! For the whole lot of them are hard-hearted and stubborn. But look, I have made you as hard and stubborn as they are. I have made you as hard as rock! So don't be afraid of them or fear their angry looks, even though they are such rebels."

-Titus 1:7-9

- List all the qualities God tells us we should not have in our character.

- List all the attributes God wants us to have in our character.

- What defines a true character according?

your thoughts

_____
_____
_____
_____
_____
_____
_____
_____
_____
_____
_____
_____
_____

If the devil can cause you to focus on your own selfish desires, he has won the battle.

talk to God

_____
_____
_____
_____
_____
_____
_____
_____
_____
_____
_____

day five

credits

- After completing this lesson, what does true character look like to you?

The credits section is designed to help you apply this week's chapter to your life. It can also be used for further discussion in a small group setting.

- Do you think your friends have noticed a change in your character this week?

- Why do you think God cares so much about our character?

- Think of one person you would like to imitate that continually demonstrates a true character. Who is it? Why?

your thoughts

_____
_____
_____
_____
_____
_____
_____
_____
_____
_____
_____
_____
_____
_____

talk to God

As a Christian, you are called by God to stand out and be different from the rest of the world.

_____
_____
_____
_____
_____
_____
_____
_____
_____
_____

day six

memory verse

- What are some key things to remember about anger?

An elder must live a blameless life because he is God's minister. He must not be arrogant or quick-tempered; he must not be a heavy drinker, violent, or greedy for money.

-Titus 1:7

- What is one thing I will commit to the Lord this week?

your thoughts

_____
_____
_____
_____
_____
_____
_____
_____
_____
_____
_____
_____
_____
_____

If you are truly serious about making a difference in your world for Christ, you must first understand and practice true character.

talk to God

_____
_____
_____
_____
_____
_____
_____
_____
_____
_____
_____
_____

day seven

review

- What has God promised me this week?

keeping it real

Having a true character allows Christ to show Himself to others through you. Let the Holy Spirit be evident in your life!

Take some time to answer these questions. It may not seem important now, but it will be awesome to look back and see how God has shaped your life.

- Does God have a command for me to obey?

- Have I done anything that I need forgiveness from God for?

- What lesson does God want me to remember this week?

- Questions about this study I need answered:

_____

_____

_____

_____

_____

_____

_____

_____

_____

_____

_____

_____

_____

_____

God desires each Christian to know His Word and memorize it.

talk to God

_____

_____

_____

_____

_____

_____

_____

_____

_____

_____

_____

_____

your journey through junior high life

memory verse section

Malachi 1:11   reputation   Chapter 1

_____

_____

_____

1 Samuel 16:7   integrity   Chapter 2

_____

_____

_____

Matthew 15:8-9   attitude   Chapter 3

_____

_____

_____

Matthew 15:18-20   honesty   Chapter 4

_____

_____

_____

Ephesians 4:26-27   anger   Chapter 5

_____

_____

_____

2 Thes. 3:10   laziness   Chapter 6

_____

_____

_____

| Proverbs 16:18 | pride | Chapter 7 |

_____
_____
_____

| Proverbs 16:27-28 | gossip | Chapter 8 |

_____
_____
_____

| Psalm 119:105-106 | decisions | Chapter 9 |

_____
_____
_____

| Joshua 1:9 | courage | Chapter 10 |

_____
_____
_____

| John 15:13 | friendship | Chapter 11 |

_____
_____
_____

| Titus 1:7 | character | Chapter 12 |

_____
_____
_____

your journey through junior high life

message notes section

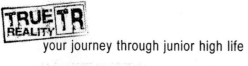

reputation

scripture passages

_____
_____
_____
_____

first key point

_____
_____
_____
_____

second key point

_____
_____
_____
_____

third key point

_____
_____
_____
_____

take away idea

_____
_____
_____
_____

integrity

scripture passages

_____
_____
_____
_____

first key point

_____
_____
_____
_____

second key point

_____
_____
_____
_____

third key point

_____
_____
_____
_____

take away idea

_____
_____
_____
_____

attitude

scripture passages

_____
_____
_____
_____

first key point

_____
_____
_____
_____

second key point

_____
_____
_____
_____

third key point

_____
_____
_____
_____

take away idea

_____
_____
_____
_____

honesty

scripture passages

_____
_____
_____
_____

first key point

_____
_____
_____
_____

second key point

_____
_____
_____

third key point

_____
_____
_____
_____

take away idea

_____
_____
_____
_____

anger

scripture passages

first key point

second key point

third key point

take away idea

laziness

scripture passages

_____

_____

_____

first key point

_____

_____

_____

second key point

_____

_____

_____

third key point

_____

_____

_____

take away idea

_____

_____

_____

pride

scripture passages

first key point

second key point

third key point

take away idea

gossip

scripture passages

_____
_____
_____
_____

first key point

_____
_____
_____
_____

second key point

_____
_____
_____
_____

third key point

_____
_____
_____
_____

take away idea

_____
_____
_____
_____

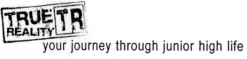
decisions

scripture passages

_____
_____
_____
_____

first key point

_____
_____
_____
_____

second key point

_____
_____
_____

third key point

_____
_____
_____
_____

take away idea

_____
_____
_____
_____

courage

scripture passages

_____
_____
_____

first key point

_____
_____
_____

second key point

_____
_____
_____

third key point

_____
_____
_____

take away idea

_____
_____
_____

friendship

scripture passages

_____
_____
_____
_____

first key point

_____
_____
_____
_____

second key point

_____
_____
_____

third key point

_____
_____
_____
_____

take away idea

_____
_____
_____
_____

character

scripture passages

_____
_____
_____
_____

first key point

_____
_____
_____
_____

second key point

_____
_____
_____
_____

third key point

_____
_____
_____
_____

take away idea

_____
_____
_____
_____

Printed in the United States
25483LVS00004B/274-285

9 780974 777252